Rays

by Martha E. H. Rustad

Consulting Editor: Gail Saunders-Smith, Ph.D.

Consultant: Jody Byrum, Science Writer,
SeaWorld Education Department

Pebble Books

an imprint of Capstone Press
Mankato, Minnesota

Pebble Books are published by Capstone Press,
1710 Roe Crest Drive, North Mankato, Minnesota 56003
www.capstonepub.com

Library of Congress Cataloging-in-Publication Data
Rustad, Martha E. H. (Martha Elizabeth Hillman), 1975–
    Rays / by Martha E. H. Rustad.
    p. cm.—(Ocean life)
    Includes bibliographical references (p. 23) and index.
    ISBN-13: 978-0-7368-0858-3 (hardcover)
    ISBN-10: 0-7368-0858-2 (hardcover)
    ISBN-13: 978-0-7368-9081-6 (softcover pbk.)
    ISBN-10: 0-7368-9081-5 (softcover pbk.)
    1. Rays (Fishes)—Juvenile literature. [1. Rays (Fishes).] I. Title. II. Series.
QL638.8 .R87 2001
597.3'5—dc21   00-009862

Summary: Simple text and photographs present rays and their behavior.

Printed in the United States of America in North Mankato, Minnesota.
052014   008171R

Note to Parents and Teachers

The Ocean Life series supports national science standards for units
on the diversity and unity of life. The series shows that animals
have features that help them live in different environments. This
book describes rays and illustrates how they live. The photographs
support early readers in understanding the text. The repetition of
words and phrases helps early readers learn new words. This book
also introduces early readers to subject-specific vocabulary words,
which are defined in the Words to Know section. Early readers may
need assistance to read some words and to use the Table of
Contents, Words to Know, Read More, Internet Sites, and
Index/Word List sections of the book.

Table of Contents

Rays are fish.

gills

Rays breathe through gills.

Rays have a flat body.

fins

Rays have large fins
that look like wings.

Most rays have a tail.

Some rays sting predators.

Rays have a mouth.

18

Rays eat clams,
crabs, and fish.

Most rays hunt for food
near the ocean floor.

Words to Know

breathe—to take oxygen into the body; a ray's gills take in oxygen from the water.

fin—a body part without bones that fish use to swim; rays have two large wing-like fins that they move up and down; rays seem to fly through the water when they swim.

fish—a cold-blooded animal that lives in water and has scales, fins, and gills

gill—a body part that fish use to breathe; a ray has gills on the bottom of its flat body.

hunt—to find and kill animals for food

mouth—a body part used to take in food; most rays have hard, flat teeth.

ocean floor—the bottom of the ocean; sand, rocks, and coral reefs cover the ocean floor; rays hunt for food there.

predator—an animal that hunts and eats other animals; sharks and seals are predators of rays.

sting—to hurt with a venomous tip; some rays have a stinging spine on their tail.

Read More

Llamas, Andreu. *Rays: Animals with an Electric Charge.* Secrets of the Animal World. Milwaukee: Gareth Stevens, 1997.

Perrine, Doug. *Sharks and Rays of the World.* Stillwater, Minn.: Voyageur Press, 1999.

Seward, Homer. *Rays.* Sea Monsters. Vero Beach, Fla.: Rourke, 1998.

Internet Sites

FactHound offers a safe, fun way to find Internet sites related to this book. All of the sites on FactHound have been researched by our staff.

Here's how:

1. Visit *www.facthound.com*
2. Type in this special code **0736808582** for age-appropriate sites. Or enter a search word related to this book for a more general search.
3. Click on the **Fetch It** button.

FactHound will fetch the best sites for you!   23

Index/Word List

Word Count: 48
Early-Intervention Level: 7

Credits
Steve Christensen, cover designer and illustrator; Kia Bielke, production designer; Kimberly Danger, photo researcher

Allan Power/Bruce Coleman Inc., 1
Graeme Teague, 18
Jay Ireland & Georgienne E. Bradley, 6, 8, 10, 12, 16, 20
Jeff Jaskolski/Innerspace Visions, cover
Norbert Wu/www.norbertwu.com, 14
Norman Owen Tomalin/Bruce Coleman Inc., 4